PRO WRESTLING LEGENDS

Steve Austin
The Story of the Wrestler They Call "Stone Cold"

Bill Goldberg

Bret Hart
The Story of the Wrestler They Call "The Hitman"

The Story of the Wrestler
They Call "Hollywood" Hulk Hogan

Randy Savage
The Story of the Wrestler They Call "Macho Man"

The Story of the Wrestler They Call "Sting"

The Story of the Wrestler They Call "The Undertaker"

Jesse Ventura
The Story of the Wrestler They Call "The Body"

CHELSEA HOUSE PUBLISHERS

Bret Hart
The Story of the Wrestler
They Call "The Hitman"

Jacqueline Mudge

Chelsea House Publishers
Philadelphia

Produced by Choptank Syndicate, Inc.

Editor and Picture Researcher: Mary Hull
Design and Production: Lisa Hochstein

CHELSEA HOUSE PUBLISHERS

Editor in Chief: Stephen Reginald
Managing Editor: James D. Gallagher
Production Manager: Pamela Loos
Art Director: Sara Davis
Director of Photography: Judy L. Hasday
Senior Production Editor: LeeAnne Gelletly
Cover Illustrator: Keith Trego

Cover Photos: WCW
Jeff Eisenberg Sports Photography

The Chelsea House World Wide Web site
address is http://www.chelseahouse.com

First Printing

1 3 5 7 9 8 6 4 2

Library of Congress Cataloging-in-Publication Data

Mudge, Jacqueline.
    Bret Hart: the story of the wrestler they call "the Hitman" / Jacqueline Mudge.
        p. cm.—(Pro wrestling legends)
    Includes bibliographical references (p.) and index.
    Summary: A biography of the professional wrestler from a well-known
wrestling family in Canada, who has won both the World Wrestling Federation
and World Championship Wrestling titles.
    ISBN 0-7910-5408-X (hard).— ISBN 0-7910-5554-X (pbk.)
    1. Hart, Bret—Juvenile literature. 2. Wrestlers—Canada—Biography—
Juvenile literature. [1. Hart, Bret. 2. Wrestlers.]   I. Title. II Series.
GV1196.H33M83 1999
796.812'092—dc21
[B]   99-38097
                                                                             CIP

Contents

CHAPTER 1
A NEW LABEL   7

CHAPTER 2
THE DUNGEON   15

CHAPTER 3
THE HART FOUNDATION   21

CHAPTER 4
ON HIS OWN   31

CHAPTER 5
BROTHER VS. BROTHER   43

CHAPTER 6
BREAKING UP IS HARD TO DO   53

Chronology   61

Further Reading   62

Index   63

1   A NEW LABEL

Bret Hart, tag team wrestler. Not Bret Hart, professional wrestler. Or Bret Hart, champion wrestler. Bret Hart, tag team wrestler. If ever there was a label that fit a man perfectly, this was it. Pigeonholing Hart was the easiest task in the world.

In 1987 Bret and his brother-in-law and tag team partner Jim Neidhart—together known as the Hart Foundation—were runners-up for *Pro Wrestling Illustrated* magazine's prestigious Tag Team of the Year award. That year, they had won their first of two World Wrestling Federation (WWF) World tag team championships and had held the belts for nine months and a day. In 1990, Hart and Neidhart won the belts again and held them for nearly seven months.

Bret Hart, tag team wrestler. It wasn't meant as a slight; it was meant as a compliment. When it came to tag team wrestling, few human beings did it better than "Hitman."

Yet, when a person thinks of himself as a whole, and a pretty decent whole at that, who wants to be known as one-half of anything?

And therein lay the problem, because in his mind and in his soul, Bret Hart knew that wasn't so. He was convinced that he, the celebrated tag team wrestler, had as much ability

---

After years of being a tag team wrestler, Bret Hart longed to succeed as a champion singles wrestler.

7

as any solo wrestler in the world. He knew that he didn't need Jim Neidhart, or any other partner, to win championships.

The time had come to prove to everybody what he already knew.

Hart was about to make one of the most difficult transitions in sports: from tag team wrestler, always reliant on a partner, to champion singles wrestler, with nobody to share the glory, and nobody to blame but yourself if something goes wrong.

The date was August 26, 1991. The event was the WWF's SummerSlam '91 pay-per-view extravaganza. The place was Madison Square Garden in New York City, arguably the world's most famous sports arena. At stake: the WWF Intercontinental title and the chance to change a label and a career forever.

Ironically, Bret's road to personal glory had begun with a tag team loss, one of the most difficult of his career.

Five months before SummerSlam—on March 24, 1991, at WrestleMania VII—the Hart Foundation had lost the WWF World tag team championship to the Nasty Boys.

That's when Hart made a crucial decision. Instead of trying to regain the tag team championship, the Hart Foundation would split up. Bret would go out on his own, with Neidhart's blessing, to begin the arduous journey through the world of singles competition.

Immediately, he was a smashing success. His list of conquered foes grew by the week. The Barbarian—pinned. Irwin R. Schyster—vanquished. Dino Bravo—crushed. The Warlord—overmatched.

Yet there was frustration, too, in Hart's campaign for solo acclaim. It came in the person of wily veteran Curt Hennig, then WWF Intercontinental champion, who had held the belt since November 19, 1990. Hennig had been around the sport for nearly as long as Hart; he debuted in 1979, while Hart made his ring debut in 1976. Like the Hitman, Hennig came from a solid wrestling background. His father, Larry Hennig, was one of the toughest men in the sport; the Hart family is the most famous wrestling family in Canada's history.

Also like Hart, Hennig was an outstanding scientific wrestler, able to mix the more artistic amateur wrestling techniques with the more rugged kicking, punching, and pounding style favored by most professionals. He knew his way around the ring. He also knew how to defend a major title, and had lost several title defenses to Hart (but retained his championship) by countout. Hennig and Hart had also fought to several time-limit draws. For Bret, a time-limit draw wasn't good enough; he needed to wear championship gold.

What Hennig might not have realized, however, was that, at least from a singles standpoint, Bret Hart was a work in progress—an unfinished gem still being polished, a man honing his repertoire. Hart was perfecting what would become his signature finishing maneuver: the "sharpshooter," his version of the scorpion deathlock, a leglock which places excruciating pressure on the victim's thighs and lower back.

"I thought the scorpion deathlock, or the sharpshooter, was something that would work for me," Bret told an interviewer in 1997. "I did

WWF Intercontinental champion Curt Hennig held the title for five months before losing it to Bret Hart at SummerSlam in 1991.

have a wicked spike piledriver from my old Stampede wrestling days, but it's hard to do on large men. Versatility has always been my strongest asset."

His strongest asset would come into play at SummerSlam '91, along with ability, perseverance, and a whole lot of family support.

Stu and Helen Hart, Bret's parents, were there at SummerSlam. So was his brother, Bruce, who had traveled to New York from Calgary, Alberta, to watch the match from ringside. What they saw was worthy of the Madison Square Garden spotlight.

The truth was, most of the sellout crowd in attendance, and the hundreds of thousands watching on pay-per-view television, had paid their money for the privilege of watching Randy Savage's marriage to his manager, Elizabeth. This was one of the rare wrestling events when a wrestling match wasn't the main event. In a way, Hart and Hennig had the responsibility of stealing the SummerSlam spotlight away from the sideshow and placing it back where it belonged: on wrestling.

They did their job.

The opening bell rang. Moments later, Bret floored Hennig with a shoulderblock, then hip-tossed him out of the ring. Hennig grimaced and held his back in pain, but managed to work his way back into the ring, where Bret scored the first two-count of the match. Although Hart would have preferred to keep the match as purely scientific as possible, he knew the smart strategy was to brawl and attack his opponent's injured back. Body slams, kicks, and punches would do the trick.

The strategy worked. Bret scored with a cross-bodyblock for one near-pinfall, then a sunset flip for another. When Hart clotheslined Hennig out of the ring, it looked like the Intercontinental champion would actually give up. Hennig stood up and started walking back to the dressing room.

Bret, however, wasn't going to let that happen. If Hennig was counted out or disqualified, he would retain the Intercontinental title. Maybe the rule wasn't fair, but it was the rule. There was nothing Bret could do but get Hennig back into the ring.

Which is exactly what he did. He grabbed Hennig by the tights and pulled him back into the ring. Indeed, Bret tugged so hard on Hennig that he nearly ripped the seat of his pants!

Realizing he wasn't going to get away easily, Hennig set down to business. Hart scored another two-count after a sunset flip, then Hennig wrested away the advantage. He whipped Bret hard into the turnbuckle, got a two-count, then dropkicked him out of the ring. When Bret returned to the ring, both men mounted the second rope and exchanged punches. Bret fell to the mat. Referee Dave Hebner threatened to disqualify Hennig. Again, Hart was alarmed. A disqualification was exactly what he didn't want.

But it could have been worse. Hennig caught Bret in a sleeperhold, one of the most dangerous wrestling moves there is. When applied properly, the sleeperhold restricts the flow of blood to the brain and causes the victim to pass out. Bret fought off its effects, then fought his way out of the hold just in time. He attempted a countermaneuver and missed, and Hennig scored another two-count.

Little by little, the match was turning against Bret, and the Intercontinental title was slipping from his grasp. Hennig was getting stronger, while Hart was getting weaker. In contrast to tag team wrestling, Bret had nowhere to turn. There was no partner to tag so he could catch his breath. He was on his own, trying to pass the greatest test of his career.

Hennig covered Bret for another pin attempt. Bret kicked out. Bret turned up the intensity of his attack and got the match back in his favor with a dizzying series of moves. He got two-counts with a vertical suplex, a small package rollup, a neckbreaker, and a flying axhandle. Bret was using every move in his repertoire. He was conducting a wrestling clinic, with Hennig as his unwilling student.

Now, Bret realized, was the time to unveil the sharpshooter. But as he applied the leglock, Hennig's manager, John Tolos, climbed onto the ring apron. Distracted, Hart chased after Tolos and belted him to the arena floor. Hennig kicked the unwary challenger from behind and gained the advantage, but Bret had one final surge of energy remaining.

With Bret down, Hennig measured him for a legdrop. Bret saw it coming. He moved away, and Hennig crashed to the mat. Hart applied the sharpshooter, and the pain shot through Hennig's thighs and up into his ailing back. Within seconds, the champion submitted.

Ringside at Madison Square Garden, Helen, Stu, and Bruce Hart jumped out of their seats.

Bret paused, then exulted.

"I don't think I've ever seen Bret wrestle better," Bruce Hart said after the match. "For months, Bret's been saying that he could become Intercontinental champion, and I never doubted him for a moment. But to beat a competitor the caliber of Hennig by submission is a feat that even I wouldn't have believed if I hadn't seen it for myself."

Of course, Bruce Hart was well aware of the label that had plagued his brother for years: tag team wrestler. But suddenly, the label had been replaced by a new one: Bret Hart, Intercontinental champion.

2   THE DUNGEON

The screams of pain coming from the basement were a constant reminder of what he'd face if he chose the life his father had chosen. Bret Hart's father, Stu, was a legend. His mother, Helen, was Stu's business partner. Together, they created the most famous wrestling family in Canada, perhaps in the entire world.

So there was never any doubt: Bret Hart would become a professional wrestler. He was surrounded by professional wrestling. He lived and breathed it. He grew up with it. He heard it.

Oh, the sounds coming from the basement! Most people have basements in their houses. The Hart family of rural Calgary, Alberta, had a dungeon.

It was in this dungeon that Stu Hart ran his training center for aspiring professional wrestlers. He was a relentless, unforgiving teacher who taught his students how to experience excruciating pain. At times, the moans of pain would echo throughout the house as Stu planted a particularly painful headlock on a helpless student.

At times, those students were his children.

"I can remember my dad squeezing me so hard that the blood vessels would break behind your eyeballs and you'd go

---

Bret, shown wrestling with his youngest brother, Owen Hart, grew up with at-home wrestling instruction provided by his father, Stu Hart, a trainer and promoter in Calgary, Alberta.

to school the next day with red eyes," Bret said in *Hitman Hart: Wrestling with Shadows*, a documentary that was broadcast in early 1999 on the Arts & Entertainment Network.

Stu Hart had learned about the rigors of life and wanted to pass along that knowledge to his son. Life isn't easy, he believed. His lessons about life were harsh, and his methods of teaching were unusual. Judging from his results, though, he must have done something right.

Born in 1915, Stu Hart grew up in a small town outside of Edmonton, Alberta. His family lived in a tent, and Stu's father hunted to put food on the table. Desperate for a way out of this harsh life in the Canadian cold, Stu took up wrestling at the local YMCA. As Stu quickly found out, life at the YMCA was no easier than it was out in the wilderness. He was humiliated by the bigger, stronger, more experienced wrestlers. He learned about pain and humility, but he never gave up.

Stu became an outstanding amateur wrestler and was chosen for the Canadian national team. After World War II ended, he moved to New York City and made his mark on the professional wrestling circuit. Stu did so well that, by the early 1950s, he had enough money to buy his own wrestling promotion in Calgary. He also bought a home and got married. Before long, Stu Hart had become synonymous with Canadian wrestling. And Helen Hart had become synonymous with maternity wards.

Smith was the first of the eight Hart boys, followed by Bruce, Keith, Wayne, and Dean. Bret was born on July 2, 1957, in Calgary, and would be followed by Ross and Owen. All eight would become professional wrestlers. All four

Hart daughters would marry professional wrestlers.

By the time Bret was six years old, he was hawking programs at his father's wrestling cards at the Stampede Pavilion, helping set up the ring, and playing introductory music for the wrestlers. Like his brothers, he easily took to sports and knew his way around the mats.

The Hart children were surrounded by wrestling. Guests at Sunday dinner included such legendary wrestlers like Abdullah the Butcher and Archie the Stomper, both of whom Stu trained. Helen tried to discourage her children from becoming professional wrestlers, but her voice went unheeded, as the post-dinner entertainment often included Stu demonstrating a move on one of his students, who more often than not were his children. There wasn't much small talk in the Hart family. Stu spent a lot of time making sure his boys were attuned to life's ups and downs. In his own unusual and sometimes violent way, he taught them about being men.

"I wouldn't be where I am without the discipline and integrity that my father instilled in me from a young age," Bret told the *Calgary Sun.* "My father was under incredible pressure to ensure that we all walked a fine line, even when he wasn't around. I was very fearful of the wrath of my father. But on account of that, I stayed out of trouble, didn't smoke or do drugs or steal. I was very susceptible to fall into the bad crowd, and I owe it to my father that I didn't."

Stu's lessons in life and wrestling often paid off, like the time Bret was in school and an older schoolmate was bullying his sister,

Georgia. Bret intervened. The kid said he wanted to fight Bret after school. Bret said, "Okay."

All day, Bret sat in class thinking about what he was going to do when school ended. He convinced himself that he could beat the bigger, older kid, even though he didn't seem to have much of a chance.

"It was like the showdown at the OK Corral," Bret recalled. "After school, my teacher even wished me luck. I walked into the alley, threw a few punches, took him down, and hammered him real good. The other kids hoisted me on their shoulders."

The scene would be recreated years later in the WWF: Bret, on shoulders of his friends, celebrating an unlikely victory.

When he was young, though, Bret wasn't sure he wanted to become a professional wrestler. He had his sights set on the silver screen. He wanted to become a movie director.

However, being a Hart, Bret mastered the fundamentals of amateur wrestling and was a standout at Ernest Manning High School in Calgary. He occasionally refereed matches for his father. He began developing his finishing move, the sharpshooter, a leglock that places incredible strain on the victim's legs and lower back. Bret's at-home training to become a professional wrestler never stopped, even while he harbored his dreams of moviemaking.

After graduating from high school, Bret took a year of broadcasting classes at Mount Royal College in Alberta. Then fate (with a little assist from Stu Hart) intervened.

In 1976, when Bret was 19, Stu was short on wrestlers for one of his cards in Calgary. He turned to his sons, and Bret answered the

Despite their mother's protests, all four of Bret's sisters married professional wrestlers. Bret's sister Diana married British Bulldog Davey Boy Smith, who trained at their father's dungeon in Calgary. Though they are brothers-in-law, Hart and Smith are also wrestling adversaries.

call. He never attended another broadcasting class. He never looked back. Bret became a professional wrestler.

Whether or not he knew it—and most likely he did—Bret had been treading this path since the day he was born, a path that would lead him to a career on the mat.

3 | THE HART FOUNDATION

I f you saw Bret Hart walking down the street, or stood next to him, you would never say to yourself, "That guy is small." At 5' 11", Bret is of slightly above-average height for a man. At 235 pounds on a muscular frame, he's certainly bigger than the average male.

Place him in a wrestling ring, however, next to guys like Hulk Hogan, Kevin Nash, or Yokozuna, and you just might ask, "How did he ever survive?"

The answer: through hard work and by paying his dues, with plenty of talent thrown in. Plus, he caught a few breaks.

In the early years, Bret teamed with two of his brothers, Smith and Keith, in both the Stampede Wrestling area in Calgary and the World Wrestling Council (WWC), which is based in Puerto Rico. Bret and Smith were quite successful. They won the WWC Caribbean tag team title in 1978. Bret and Keith were also quite successful. They won the Stampede International tag team title on several occasions.

In November 1978, Bret won his first singles title, the British Commonwealth mid-heavyweight title, leading to a feud that would be rekindled in the mid-1980s and last for the rest of the decade. The feud was with Davey Boy Smith, who would marry Bret's sister Diana. Bret and Davey Boy

---

To reach out to fans and increase his popularity as a pro wrestler, Bret had to overcome his natural shyness and develop the persona of the Hitman.

Smith were two of the most talented mat wrestlers in North America and their matches thrilled the fans in Calgary with fast action and a wide variety of maneuvers.

Over the course of his six-plus years in Stampede, Bret won six North American heavyweight titles.

Unfortunately for Bret, he had one shortcoming: he was terribly shy. This might not have mattered in any other sport, but wrestling is different from any other sport. An important part of a professional wrestler's job is giving televised interviews. More than any other sport, professional wrestling demands that its athletes have strong, colorful personalities. The wrestlers who don't come off well on TV rarely get the promotional push needed to earn them title opportunities.

Bret, however, was no ham. Remember, it was behind the camera that he wanted to make his career in Hollywood, not in front of it.

That's when Bret hit upon an idea. Rather than expressing himself with wild tirades and outlandish stunts, he would give himself a colorful nickname. He took the nickname from boxer Tommy "the Hitman" Hearns. Bret decided that he, too, would be the Hitman.

In an attempt to hide his nervousness during interviews, Bret started wearing dark wraparound sunglasses with colorful frames. The nickname, the glasses, and the dark, slicked-back hair adorned Bret with a persona that words alone could never have given him.

Then, in 1984, Stu Hart's business transaction with Vince McMahon Jr. gave Bret his next big break. Attendance in the Alberta area was down and the Stampede promotion was struggling. When Stu Hart sold his territory to McMahon, the owner of the WWF, Bret's life was changed forever. Suddenly, in 1984, Bret was a member of the largest federation in North America.

Although WWF fans appreciated Bret's hardworking style, the Hitman had a hard time grabbing their attention. Those were the days of Hulkamania. Hogan had kicked and punched his way to the WWF World title in 1984, and other wrestlers were following his example. Meanwhile, Bret was plugging along, trying to get people to notice his mat skills. Few cared. To most people, amateur-style wrestling was boring.

In 1985, wrestling was undergoing a dramatic change, and Bret was left behind. It was the era of the rock 'n' wrestling connection, a time when pop singer Cyndi Lauper and actor Mr. T were major players at WrestleMania I. Glitz, glamour, and the sideshow were more important than wrestling. No matter how well Bret wrestled, no matter how hard he tried, he couldn't move up in the ranks. He was too bland.

Bret did have his moments, though. At WrestleMania II on April 7, 1986, he nearly won a 20-man battle royal that included such greats as Andre the Giant, the Iron Sheik, and two-time former WWF World champion Bruno Sammartino. Bret was the last man eliminated by Andre, who won the match.

The answer to Bret's image problem turned out to be a pencil-thin man who had long, black hair, wore outrageous suits, carried a megaphone, and spoke like a crazed carnival barker. His name was Jimmy Hart, and he was of no

French-Canadian brothers Jacques and Raymond Rougeau were one of the Hart Foundation's biggest rivals. Here Jacques wrestles Bret for the tag team championship.

relation to Bret. Jimmy Hart—known as "the Mouth of the South"—instantly recognized Bret's potential and decided to team him with Bret's brother-in-law, Jim "the Anvil" Neidhart. The Hart Foundation was born.

The duo was an instant success. Combining Bret's scientific skill and speed with Neidhart's power and brutality was a stroke of brilliance. The package was completed by Jimmy Hart, whose obnoxious, interfering style made it clear to everyone who watched that the Hart Foundation didn't care how it won. They became one of the great rulebreaking tag teams of the 1980s.

The Hart Foundation wasted no time setting its sights on the WWF World tag team champions, the British Bulldogs—the team of Davey Boy Smith and Dynamite Kid.

The Hart Foundation struck gold in Tampa, Florida, on January 26, 1987, less than a year after they had been formed. They beat the Bulldogs for the WWF World tag team title in a controversial match. Hart and Neidhart were probably good enough to win on their own, but Jimmy Hart wasn't taking any chances. He paid off referee Danny Davis, who conveniently ignored Hart's interference and made a fast count on the final pin attempt.

Now the Hart Foundation really had the public's attention. Not only had its wrestlers won the World tag team championship, but they had bribed a referee! No longer did Bret and Neidhart seem so bland and boring.

The Bulldogs were enraged by Davis's actions and wanted a way to settle the score. The WWF ordered a six-man tag team match for WrestleMania III that would pit the Bulldogs and Tito Santana against the Hart Foundation and Davis. The referee-turned-rulebreaker played the key role in the match when he grabbed Jimmy Hart's megaphone and hit Davey Boy Smith, then pinned Smith for the victory.

The Hart Foundation appeared to have lost the belts to Jacques and Raymond Rougeau—two French-Canadian brothers—on September

26, 1987, in Montreal. Raymond Rougeau grabbed Jimmy Hart's megaphone and hit Bret, then covered him for the pin. But as the video-tape of the match proved, Bret was not the legal man in the ring; Neidhart had never tagged out. WWF President Jack Tunney reversed the deci-sion and gave the belts back to the Hart Foundation.

It seemed as if Hart and Neidhart could do no wrong. When they cheated, they got away with it. When another team cheated, that team was caught. The fans' hatred for the Hart Foundation grew more intense by the day. Bret was a full-fledged rulebreaker, and an egotisti-cal one, at that. He seemed genuinely proud of his good looks and muscular body. Being a champion had changed the Hitman.

The Harts finally lost the belts on October 27, 1987, to Rick Martel and Tito Santana, a team known as Strike Force. But that didn't stop the readers of *Pro Wrestling Illustrated* magazine from voting the Hart Foundation as first runners-up for Tag Team of the Year. Jimmy Hart was voted Manager of the Year.

At the Royal Rumble on January 24, 1988, Bret gave another indication that he could be a force to be reckoned with in the WWF singles ranks.

The Royal Rumble is an unusual event. It's similar to a battle royal in that it involves 30 men and the goal is to be the last man stand-ing. The difference between the Rumble and an ordinary battle royal is that the wrestlers enter the ring one at a time. The match starts with two men. After a few minutes, another man enters, then a few minutes later another, and so on. To win, a wrestler needs either the luck

*Jim "the Anvil"
Neidhart and Bret
"Hitman" Hart of the
Hart Foundation,
receive their WWF
World tag team
championship belts.*

of the draw (the later he enters, the better chance he has to win) or incredible stamina.

Bret didn't have the luck of the draw. He didn't win. But he lasted an incredible 36 minutes, more than any other competitor, and eliminated several men while constantly fending off his own elimination. Bret's performance was proof of his talent, stamina, and ability as a singles wrestler.

At WrestleMania IV on March 27, 1988, Bret began his transformation from rulebreaker to wrestling hero. Bret and Bad News Brown, an old rival from Calgary, were the last two men standing in a 20-man battle royal. Brown attacked Bret from behind and dumped him over the top rope, instantly converting Bret from rulebreaker to fan favorite. Neidhart, too, suddenly became liked by the fans.

Jimmy Hart, however, was not along for the ride. He had no interest in doing things right or getting cheered. In a cruel act of deception, Jimmy Hart sold one of the Hart Foundation's title shots to the Rougeau brothers. When Bret and Neidhart found out about this, they immediately confronted and dumped their manager.

The Hart Foundation feuded with the Rougeaus, but Jimmy Hart was their real target. At the 1989 Royal Rumble, Bret, Neidhart, and Hacksaw Duggan defeated the Rougeaus and Dino Bravo in a six-man tag team match.

These were difficult times for Bret and Neidhart. They continued to win, but they rarely received title shots. Finally, after more than two years as fan favorites, their dedication paid off. At SummerSlam '90 on August 27, 1990, the Hart Foundation won a best-of-three falls match against Demolition, a tag team managed by Jimmy Hart, to win the belts.

Bret and Neidhart were fortunate to retain the title for as long as they did. One of the most controversial tag team matches in WWF history took place on October 30, 1990, in Fort Wayne, Indiana, between the Harts and the Rockers, the team of Marty Jannetty and Shawn Michaels.

It was an unusual match that marked one of the few times in WWF history that two fan-favorite teams faced each other for the belts.

The fans at the Coliseum didn't know who to root for. In the first fall of this best-of-three-falls match, Jannetty reversed a sunset flip and pinned Bret. In the second fall, Hart used his clothesline to pin Michaels. During that fall, however, the top rope was knocked off the cornerpost, causing the ring to sag. The match continued and, in the third fall, Jannetty pinned Hart, apparently to win the belts.

The next day, WWF president Jack Tunney reviewed the tapes and rescinded the Rockers' victory because the ropes had been rendered unusable for the last eight minutes of the match. The Hart Foundation was still the WWF World champion tag team.

Unfortunately, there wasn't much time to celebrate. On November 21, 1990, Bret's older brother, Dean, died in Calgary of a kidney disease. Distraught, Bret made the tough decision to wrestle the following night at the Survivor Series and dedicated his match to Dean. But Bret's team lost to Ted DiBiase's Million-Dollar Team when Bret was pinned by DiBiase.

On March 24, 1991, at WrestleMania VII, the Nasty Boys, under the guidance of Jimmy Hart, defeated Bret and Neidhart, ending their seven-month title reign.

Rather than going right back after the Nasty Boys, Bret took a step back and examined his career. Neidhart did the same. They decided to go their separate ways. Bret would pursue the rest of his dreams on his own. The Hart Foundation was history. And history was about to be made.

4 ON HIS OWN

Bret was disappointed that the Hart Foundation's run had ended, but he was confident in his ability as a singles wrestler. He knew this time would be different from his first try as a singles wrestler in the WWF. Back in 1985, not too many people knew who he was. Now, he was a superstar, thanks to his success with Jim Neidhart. Back in 1985, glitz, glamour, and brawling was the name of the game. In 1990, things were starting to change. The rock 'n' wrestling era was over. People were once again appreciating the sport's subtler qualities.

Neidhart went into semi-retirement to rest injuries he had suffered over the years. Bret, who certainly could have used the rest, never missed a beat. His charge to the top of the WWF was seamless and sensational. Nobody was really surprised when he beat Curt Hennig for the Intercontinental title on August 26, 1991, at Madison Square Garden.

Bret was receiving international acclaim. The fans loved him. He had never wrestled better. His sharpshooter move was stunningly effective; opponents couldn't escape it no matter how hard they tried. Bret was poised and confident in interviews, declaring himself the "excellence of execution" and "the best there is, the best there ever was, and the best there ever

---

After claiming two WWF World tag team titles, Hart launched a successful singles career, first winning the WWF Intercontinental championship and later becoming a WWF World heavyweight champion several times.

will be." He was tireless, capable of outlasting wrestlers in the best physical condition. Two weeks after his Intercontinental title victory, Bret entered the WWF's annual King of the Ring tournament and defeated three opponents in one day to become King of the Ring.

Always lurking in the background, however, was Jimmy Hart, Bret's former manager. The Mouth of the South hadn't relented in his desire to destroy and embarrass the Hitman, and in late 1991, he sent his new charge, the Mountie, after Bret. The Mountie was an unusual character. He mimicked the Royal Canadian National Police, further enraging Bret, who was proud of his Canadian heritage. In reality, the Mountie wasn't a Mountie at all. In fact, he regularly broke the rules and flaunted his disrespect for authority.

At first, the Mountie was no match for Bret. One night, Bret needed only three seconds, the bare minimum in wrestling, to pin him. But the Mountie held the upper hand when he and Bret stepped into the ring on January 17, 1992, just two days before their scheduled title clash at the Royal Rumble. Bret was suffering from the flu and battling dehydration. He had a 104-degree fever. WWF officials gave him the opportunity to back out of the match, but Bret decided to honor his commitment. He might as well have just handed the Mountie the belt. In what appeared to be a shocking upset (but really wasn't, given Bret's physical condition), the Mountie beat him for the Intercontinental title.

At the Royal Rumble, Roddy Piper, Bret's friend and another wrestling legend, took Bret's place and won the title from the Mountie. Right away, Bret demanded a title match. Piper hesitated. He did not want to go up against Hart, one of his favorite wrestlers. Bret refused to take no for an answer. He desperately wanted to win back the belt. Bret displayed an aggressiveness that bordered on outright rulebreaking and demanded matches until Piper could no longer refuse.

They met at WrestleMania VII on April 5 at the Hoosier Dome in Indianapolis, Indiana. When the bell rang and the match began, Bret and Piper stared each other down, gazing into each other's eyes with frightening intensity. They battled inside and outside of the ring, bloodying each other's faces and flooring each other with brutal clotheslines. Piper, displaying his old rulebreaking tactics, threw Bret into the referee, clotheslined him out of the ring, and slammed his head into the ring steps. When the action returned to the ring, Piper threatened to smash Bret with the timekeeper's bell, but backed off and placed Bret in a sleeperhold.

Bret responded with a brilliant display of counterwrestling. He mounted the turnbuckle and pushed off, sending Piper to the mat. Still trapped in the sleeper, Bret flipped backwards and scored the pin to regain the belt.

By winning the Intercontinental title for a second time, and by beating a veteran champion, Bret had proven to the world that he was an elite singles wrestler. He celebrated the victory by dedicating his title defenses to his father, who had recently turned 76.

Bret couldn't have been more impressive. He humbled Shawn Michaels, another former tag team wrestler trying to make a name for himself in the singles ranks. Bret was annoyed

The largest challenger Hart met in defense of his World title was 500-pound Yokozuna, who, despite his massive size, resorted to cheating in order to pin Bret.

by Michaels's egotism and bragging, and took out his frustrations by pinning "the Heartbreak Kid" several times. Then, in early June, the WWF announced that Bret would defend his title against Davey Boy Smith at SummerSlam '92.

The very idea of this match captured the imagination. Bret and Davey Boy had been rivals in the feud between the Hart Foundation and the British Bulldogs. Bret's sister, Diana, was married to Davey Boy. Both she and Bret's mother expressed misgivings about the match. Both men insisted they were family outside the ring and foes within it. And Davey Boy, who was born in Leeds, England, would have the fans on his side: SummerSlam '92 would be held in front of a sellout crowd at Wembley Stadium in London.

The match lived up to its advance billing and would be voted Match of the Year by the readers of *Pro Wrestling Illustrated* magazine. For the first time in years, Bret was greeted by a loud chorus of boos as he made his way to the ring. He defiantly kissed the belt, then got down to business with his brother-in-law, who was suddenly his staunchest rival.

The match was a clinic in scientific excellence. Both men were at their very best. Smith nearly pinned Bret with a running powerslam, then Bret maneuvered Smith into a sharpshooter. Davey Boy had no chance of escaping it, but he reached out and grabbed the bottom rope, forcing Bret to release the hold. Smith responded with a superplex that sent Bret flying backwards to the mat. Bret kicked out in time, but seconds later, Davey Boy covered Bret for the pin.

Davey Boy couldn't believe he had won. As the crowd cheered, he stared at the belt for several seconds. Then he offered to shake Bret's hand. Bret refused before graciously embracing his brother-in-law. Then Diana Smith entered the ring and joined her husband and brother in the lengthy celebration.

As had become his habit, Bret never looked back. He never thought about what he could have done to beat Davey Boy, and he didn't demand rematches. Instead, he set his sights on a new, loftier goal: winning the WWF World heavyweight championship from Ric Flair.

At first, Bret struggled against Flair, who as an eight-time former National Wrestling

Alliance (NWA) World champion, knew how to defend a title. But Bret's road to the top of the wrestling world was neither long nor hard.

The date: October 12, 1992.

The scene: Saskatoon, Saskatchewan, in the Canadian west.

Flair controlled the first 10 minutes of the match, but Bret escaped Flair's figure-four leglock. It was a remarkable turn of events. Few people have ever escaped Flair's famed figure-four. The reversal changed the course of the match.

Flair kept applying his figure-four and Bret kept reversing it. The two men battled in an incredible display of stamina, but with 25 minutes gone in the match, Flair looked far more tired than Bret. With Flair exhausted and unable to mount an offensive, Hart blasted Flair with a superplex suplex from atop the corner turnbuckle, then forced him to submit to a sharpshooter.

The crowd was exultant. Bret could hardly believe it when a WWF official handed him the World championship belt, one of wrestling's greatest prizes.

"This is the greatest day of my life," Bret told the crowd. "I've got a lot to be thankful for and I am proud to be WWF champion. This is an example of hard work and perseverance paying off. I have been working toward this since I was a kid, and now I have reached the pinnacle."

Bret had become a wrestling immortal. He was the first person in history to win the WWF World, Intercontinental, and World tag team titles. He had done something Hulk Hogan and Bruno Sammartino had never done. His excellence was indisputable.

Bret was a proud champion who defended the title honorably against all challengers. Michaels, Razor Ramon, Ted DiBiase, and Kamala all fell prey to Hart. Unlike many champions, who reach their peak when they win the belt, Bret kept getting better. Flair was relentless in his pursuit of the title. Bret was more relentless in his desire to keep it. Ramon got the shot against Bret at the 1993 Royal Rumble. With his family sitting at ringside, Bret forced the bigger, stronger Ramon to submit.

"Outstanding!" Stu Hart said after the match. "I have never been more proud of Bret."

It is the truth of being champion, however, that the challenges never get easier. Dispose of one opponent and there's always another bigger, stronger, tougher man standing right behind him, waiting for his chance. When Yokozuna, who weighed over 500 pounds, won the Royal Rumble to earn a shot at the World title at WrestleMania IX, Bret knew he would face a dire challenge. Then Yokozuna upped the ante by attacking Hart during the contract signing for the match.

Over the following months, Bret proved his ability to beat big men by humbling Ramon and Bam Bam Bigelow and beating Yokozuna by pinfall, countout, or disqualification in every one of their matches. Although Yokozuna was several hundred pounds larger, Bret was the superior all-around wrestler. The one thing Yokozuna had on his side was Mr. Fuji, the devious manager who relished using foreign objects.

Bret wrestled brilliantly in his WrestleMania IX showdown with Yokozuna at Caesar's Palace in Las Vegas. The advantage switched several times. Yokozuna choked Bret on the ropes. Bret recovered and went for the pin, but Yokozuna escaped. Bret assaulted Yokozuna with clotheslines. Yokozuna wrapped up Bret in a waistlock and easily lifted him off the mat. The former Sumo wrestler tried to smash Bret's face into the exposed metal turnbuckle, but Bret blocked the move and slammed Yokozuna into the corner.

Realizing he had a chance to win the match, Bret put Yokozuna into a sharpshooter. Yokozuna was ready to submit when Mr. Fuji dipped into his pocket, pulled out a handful of salt, and flung the salt in Bret's eyes.

The sting of the salt striking his eyes caused Bret to draw back in pain. Seizing the sudden advantage, Yokozuna hooked Bret's leg for the pin. Bret's World title reign was over after five months and 23 days, and it had ended in the most controversial way possible. Yokozuna and Fuji had cheated.

As the disappointed crowd got up to leave, Hulk Hogan ran out of the dressing room to argue with referee Dave Hebner and console Bret. Meanwhile, Mr. Fuji grabbed the ring microphone and issued an on-the-spot challenge to Hogan. After some prodding from Hart and the crowd, Hogan accepted the challenge.

Twenty-five seconds later, Hogan had pinned Yokozuna after Fuji's salt-throwing misfired.

The title had changed hands twice within minutes.

Even worse for Bret, he was no longer the top contender to the World title. That distinction belonged to Yokozuna.

"When the salt was thrown, it was a sense of relief," Bret said. "I had no doubt the decision, at that point, would be in my favor by way of

Jerry "the King" Lawler tries to blind Hart by throwing an unknown substance into his eyes. In 1993 Jerry Lawler began feuding with Hart, playing tricks on him and insulting his family. Lawler's antics distracted Bret, making it hard for him to focus on his goal of regaining the World title.

disqualification. Nobody in their right mind could award the title to someone after the manager did something like that. Once I realized that I had been shafted, had the belt stolen away, I didn't think the decision would last. Then, about an hour later, it become obvious that nobody was going to do anything about it. If Hulk Hogan would've been any kind of hero, the type I always thought he was, I would've assumed he would not have accepted the title."

Most people expected Hogan to graciously offer title shots to Bret. After all, hadn't Bret told Hogan to accept Mr. Fuji's impromptu challenge? Yokozuna's original victory over Bret was highly controversial. Hogan knew that. He had run out to protest the outcome.

Hogan, however, never offered Hart a title shot. They didn't even speak. In fact, for 10 weeks, Hogan didn't once defend the belt. Hart was incensed; he never imagined the impromptu match was for the title. So, he might have been pleased when Yokozuna regained the belt in Hogan's first title defense.

"To say I'm bitter is an understatement," Bret said.

He plugged on. He won his second King of the Ring on June 13, 1993, by pinning Razor Ramon, Curt Hennig, and Bam Bam Bigelow. The victory incurred the wrath of Jerry "the King" Lawler, who considered himself to be the King of the Ring. During the coronation ceremonies, Lawler stormed the ring and ordered Bret to kiss his feet. When Bret refused. Lawler hit him with a scepter, broke Bret's crown, and choked him.

Lawler, a longtime favorite in Memphis, Tennessee, underwent a transformation whenever he wrestled in the WWF. He was a hated rulebreaker, and Bret had become his chief target. He ridiculed and insulted Bret's family.

The feud was a massive distraction for Bret. Rather than going after Yokozuna and the World title, he focused all of his energy on Lawler. Both men were consumed by the feud. Lawler used every trick in the book to get Bret angry. Bret, along with his brother, Owen, even went so far as to chase after Lawler in the United

States Wrestling Alliance (USWA), Lawler's home territory. At SummerSlam '93, Lawler deceived Bret into thinking he was injured. When Bret and Lawler finally wrestled, Bret refused to release his sharpshooter, even after Lawler had submitted. The referee reversed the decision and awarded the match to Lawler.

Lawler had no limit to how low he would stoop to destroy Bret. He was both relentless and ruthless.

"Where is this going to end?" Bret asked. "It could get even uglier. Maybe I will have to end his career, to cripple him. I don't like to think along those terms, but it's like I'm being pushed in that direction."

He kept getting pushed, not only by Lawler, but by another person, one he never could have dreamed would be his enemy.

5 BROTHER VS. BROTHER

Bret enjoyed being in the same federation as his younger brother, Owen. They'd travel together, get together after matches, and enjoy the camaraderie that exists between two brothers. Though they were often opponents in the ring, they were family outside of it.

Bret was looking forward to teaming with three of his brothers, Owen, Keith, and Bruce, in a match against Shawn Michaels, the Black Knight, the Red Knight, and the Blue Knight (all masked wrestlers hired by Jerry Lawler) in an elimination match at the 1993 Survivor Series.

It turned into a family nightmare.

During the match, Michaels escaped a series of pin attempts by Bret and Owen, then raked his fingers across Bret's face. Owen tagged in and continued the attack while Bret walked toward his team's corner. When Owen rebounded off the ropes, he mistakenly knocked Bret off the ring apron and into the metal ring barrier. Michaels covered Owen for the pin, eliminating the youngest Hart from the match.

Owen was furious at his brother. As Keith and Bruce tended to Bret, Owen leaned over the ropes and yelled, "What are you doing?" When Keith and Bruce ignored him, Owen mumbled, "What about me?" and walked back to the dressing room.

An ecstatic Bret Hart holds up the championship belt after regaining the WWF World title from Yokozuna at Wrestlemania X on March 20, 1994, at Madison Square Garden.

Brothers Bret and
Owen Hart wrestled
in the opening match
of Wrestlemania X
at Madison Square
Garden. Owen won
the match, but Bret
overshadowed his
brother later in the
evening by capturing
his second WWF
World title.

Bret got back on his feet and the Harts went on to win the match. As Keith, Bruce, and Bret celebrated, Owen returned to the ring. As his parents watched at ringside, Owen pushed Bret to the mat and screamed, "I don't need you!"

Stu Hart tried to reconcile his sons, but Owen was too angry. He turned to his father and yelled, "Why do those guys always have to get in the way? I never get any recognition!"

Eventually, Owen and Bret talked things over and agreed to form a tag team. They wrestled WWF World tag team champions the Quebecers at the 1994 Royal Rumble in January.

Bret got hurt late in the match when he was thrown out of the ring and his left leg struck the guard rail. In obvious pain for the rest of the match, Bret was no match for the Quebecers' unforgiving attack. Owen tried to intervene, but for reasons that never became clear, Bret tried to wrestle the rest of the match by himself, even though Owen kept trying to tag in. Although Bret eventually placed Pierre in his sharpshooter, the referee stopped the match because Bret appeared to be in extreme pain. The strain of applying the sharpshooter was too much for Bret to withstand. Owen was angry at Bret.

"Why didn't you tag me?" Owen screamed. "I knew your leg was hurt, but all you had to do was tag me! But no, you're too . . . selfish!"

When Bret got up, Owen kicked him in the injured knee and left the ring. WWF officials arrived to carry Bret away on a stretcher while Owen appeared on the giant TV screen in the arena and berated his brother.

Although he was hurt, Bret competed in the Royal Rumble later in the evening. He and Lex Luger were the last two men remaining when they both got tangled in the ropes and went over the top. They hit the arena floor at the same time. Even slow-motion videotape replays couldn't distinguish which man had hit the floor first. WWF President Jack Tunney declared them cowinners and gave both Luger and Bret title shots at WrestleMania X.

Owen and Bret met in the opening match of WrestleMania X at Madison Square Garden in New York. Owen spent most of this classic match working on Bret's injured left leg. Three times, Owen slammed Bret's knee into the cornerpost. Then Owen, applied a sharpshooter on Bret's left leg. With 20:21 gone, Owen completed the upset by rolling up his brother for the pin.

"I'm up on Cloud Nine!" Owen exulted. "Maybe now I'll start getting the recognition I deserve, because I'm the better man, Bret. I beat you!"

But before the night ended, Owen was right back in Bret's shadow. Because of the result at the Royal Rumble, both Luger and Hart received title shots at WrestleMania X. Luger went first and lost to Yokozuna by disqualification. Bret, limping to the ring on a badly injured leg, got the second shot at Yokozuna in the final match of the night.

In an attempt to finish off Bret, Yokozuna hurled his massive body toward the Hitman from the second rope. Bret rolled out of the way, and Yokozuna crashed onto the mat. Bret, though dazed, crawled over, hooked Yokozuna's leg, and got the three-count for his second WWF World title.

As WWF champion, Bret frequently faced challenges from his brother, Owen, and the WWF promoted the feud between the two.

At the 1994 King of the Ring pay-per-view, Bret had his old partner, Jim Neidhart, in his corner for a match against Intercontinental champion Diesel. Neidhart's interference enabled Diesel to win the match, but Bret retained the belt. As Neidhart returned to the dressing room, Diesel and Shawn Michaels brutalized Bret. Nobody knew until later why Neidhart had left Bret behind.

The answer was revealed in the King of the Ring finals between Owen and Razor Ramon.

Riding on the shoulders of Lex Luger and Razor Ramon, Bret Hart celebrates his WWF World title victory at Wrestlemania X.

When Neidhart ran out to the ring, everyone assumed he was there to help Ramon. He wasn't. Neidhart clotheslined Ramon and rammed him into the cornerpost. Owen easily finished off Ramon for the pin to become the King of the Ring.

"I can't believe what just happened," Bret told the television audience. "I don't have any comment."

Owen had a comment. He gloated. "Everybody, I'm the King of the Ring!" he shouted.

The WWF scheduled a steel cage match between Owen and Bret for SummerSlam '94.

Bret had his brother Bruce in his corner. Owen had Neidhart in his corner. The feud merely intensified when Davey Boy Smith interfered on Bret's behalf. Now it was brother and brother-in-law vs. brother and brother-in-law.

Meanwhile, Bob Backlund, a former WWF World champion who once owned a clean-cut image, had turned into a crazed rulebreaker. Backlund was attacking WWF fan favorites left and right, and he finally got around to challenging Bret for the World title. They met at the 1994 Survivor Series. Davey Boy stood in Bret's corner. Owen stood in Backlund's corner for this submission match. Both cornermen held a white towel which they were to throw into the ring if their man wanted to give up.

Former WWF World champion Bob Backlund wrestled the World title away from Bret at the 1994 Survivor Series.

Nothing went right for Bret. Davey Boy was rendered unconscious during the match when he hit his head on the steps leading to the ring. Seconds later, Backlund applied his "chicken wing" armlock finisher, and Bret screamed in pain.

At ringside, Stu and Helen Hart could barely stand to watch. Owen acted as if he couldn't stand to watch, either.

Finally, Helen walked to ringside, grabbed the towel, and tossed it between the ropes. The submission was registered. Backlund was the new World champion.

Following his loss to Backlund, Bret entered the

most unproductive period of his career. Over the next 361 days, he would receive only two title shots. The feuds with his brother and Lawler consumed most of his time, but served only to push him further beyond the fringes of title contention and widen the rift that tore apart his family.

Bret finally got back on the title track at the In Your House pay-per-view on October 22, 1995, when he interfered in a match, causing World champion Diesel to lose by disqualification to Davey Boy Smith. The WWF wasted no time scheduling a match between Bret and Diesel at the 1995 Survivor Series.

It was a classic confrontation pitting a scientific wrestler, the relatively diminutive Hart, against the huge Diesel, who stands 7' and weighs 356 pounds. Bret appeared to be doomed to defeat when Diesel sent him crashing through the announcers' table, then prepared to deliver his finishing move, the "jackknife" power bomb, in which he slams his opponent shoulder-first to the mat. But Bret was playing possum. He wasn't really hurt. Bret rolled up an unwary Diesel for the pin at 24:42 to become the WWF's second three-time World champion.

Despite his happiness over regaining the belt, Bret seemed to be losing his heart for wrestling. Hollywood beckoned. He guest-starred on the TV series *Lonesome Dove* and received positive reviews. Bret was enjoying himself in front of the camera—more, perhaps, than he was enjoying himself in the ring.

He narrowly escaped his World title defense against The Undertaker at the 1996 Royal Rumble when Diesel interfered. At In Your

House VI, on February 18, 1996, The Under-taker's interference prevented Diesel from beating Bret for the belt.

Weeks before WrestleMania XIII and his showdown with Shawn Michaels, Bret made a stunning announcement: he would be cutting back his wrestling schedule after the card.

The Michaels vs. Hart match at Wrestle-Mania XIII was an epic that would win Match of the Year honors by a wide margin. WWF president Jack Tunney had ordered a 60-minute match in which the man with the most pins within that time would be the winner. Despite 15 two-counts, there were no pins in the first 60 minutes. The match went into sudden-death

Though Diesel was 13 inches taller and 121 pounds heavier than Hart, he was unable to defend his title against the Hitman at the 1995 Survivor Series. By defeating Diesel, Hart became the second wrestler in the WWF to win a third World championship.

overtime. Michaels connected with a high kick to Bret's face and scored the pin after 61 minutes, 52 seconds of grueling action.

A few weeks later, Bret decided it was time for a long vacation. He went home to Calgary and got reacquainted with his wife, Julie, and his children, Dallas, Black, Jade, and Alexandra. He enjoyed watching the Calgary Hitmen, the Canadian junior hockey team he owned with seven other people. For the first time in his life, he thought about life beyond the squared circle.

"Many, many years ago when I got into wrestling, I set out to accomplish a lot of things," Bret said in an interview with *Pro Wrestling Illustrated* magazine. "In a lot of areas, I've accomplished everything I could have ever hoped to. Of course, I've had other dreams and goals I'd like to fulfill, too. I would like to do more cartoons. I used to be a great cartoonist and I guess I still am. I would like to possibly write a book, not necessarily on wrestling, either. I wouldn't mind doing a comic strip or a comic book. I've had my cartoons published in the *Calgary Sun* . . . I have to have a reason and a desire to come back."

Eight months later, in November 1996, Bret found a reason. He recaptured the desire. He did come back—as a changed man.

6 BREAKING UP IS HARD TO DO

A man like Bret "Hitman" Hart, a traditionalist who was brought up believing in the ethics of fair play, can't possibly be expected to adjust to the topsy-turvy wrestling world of the late-1990s. Can he?

Spend your life walking the straight-and-narrow path and, every once in a while, the world is going to cross right in front of you and just keep on going, leaving you behind.

That's what happened to Bret. The wrestling world had changed several times since Bret arrived in the WWF in 1984. In late 1996, it changed again.

More specifically, the taste of the fans changed. In the past, arrogant and often obscene rulebreakers like Shawn Michaels and Steve Austin had been hated by the fans. Somehow, though, two men who showed disdain for their boss, cursed, drank, and showered obscenities upon opposing wrestlers had become the most popular wrestlers in the world.

Bret didn't know what to do, so he continued to wrestle as best he could. Austin's cheating allowed him to win the 1997 Royal Rumble, after eliminating Bret, who was the last of his opponents left in the ring. But when Shawn Michaels, who had won the title at the Royal Rumble, vacated the belt

After leaving the WWF, Bret joined WCW and became a member of the rulebreaking clique of wrestlers known as the New World Order.

because of a knee injury, WWF president Gorilla Monsoon ordered a four-way match to fill the vacancy.

The participants were Bret, Austin, Big Van Vader, and The Undertaker. The only way to eliminate an opponent was to pin him, force him to submit, or throw him over the top rope. Austin was the first man eliminated. Big Van Vader went next. The match came down to Bret and The Undertaker. Austin remained on the scene and prevented The Undertaker from eliminating Bret. Then Bret clotheslined The Undertaker over the top rope for the victory.

"This victory is for me," he said. "I showed I'm still the best there is, and I'll prove it in the ring every night if I have to."

The title reign lasted one day. One night later at *Monday Night Raw*, Sid Vicious beat Bret when Austin interfered. Bret complained. The fans started perceiving him as a whiner. A week before WrestleMania XIII, Bret again faced Vicious, this time in a cage match. Vicious won, thanks to The Undertaker's interference. When WWF owner/announcer Vince McMahon tried to interview him, Bret threw McMahon to the mat. Again, Bret complained bitterly about the interference.

When Bret was introduced at WrestleMania XIII, the fans' cheers were mixed with boos. Bret won the match with his sharpshooter. With Austin lying unconscious on the mat, Bret continued his assault. The boos got louder. Bret didn't care.

The way Bret explained it in the documentary film *Wrestling with Shadows*, he hadn't changed. The fans had changed. He was the same Hitman of old. He hadn't betrayed the fans; the fans had betrayed him by embracing wrestlers who were bad role models.

"I loved being a hero to people around the world," Bret said. "In India, where these kids showed up and waited a whole afternoon for me just to come to the school. It was like a God coming to the school. They really believed in you."

Bret realized the painful truth: the American fans didn't believe in him anymore. So he stopped believing in them.

At *Monday Night Raw* on March 24, 1997, Bret told the fans what he thought of them. He criticized American wrestling fans for not respecting his dignity, poise, and class, and for siding with men like Michaels.

"You U.S. fans don't respect me," Hart said as the boos rained down from the rafters. "Well, the fact is, I don't respect you. You don't deserve it."

It was shocking and it was heartfelt. The following week, Bret came to the ring and stopped Davey Boy Smith from choking Owen.

"You guys shouldn't be fighting," Bret told them. "The three of us need to join together for the sake of the family."

As tears streamed down Owen's face, Bret urged them to join forces against Austin, Michaels, the WWF, and American wrestling fans. Owen and Davey Boy accepted the invitation, and the new Hart Foundation

Bret Hart's belief in the importance of fair play and good role models was soured by wrestling fans who idolized rulebreakers and despised the good guys. Eventually, Bret became a rule-breaker himself and allowed outside interference to help him defeat The Undertaker for his fifth WWF World title in 1997.

was born. A few weeks later, Brian Pillman and Jim Neidhart joined the group.

Bret's feud with Austin got hotter. Austin used a chair to injure Bret's knee and arm. While sidelined with the injuries, which took longer than he expected to heal, Bret continued his tirades against the United States. He was loved on the Canadian side of the border, where his anti-American tirades played to the crowd, and hated on the U.S. side.

When Bret returned, he went after The Undertaker, who had won the belt from Vicious at WrestleMania XIII on March 23, 1997. They signed for a match at SummerSlam '97. If Bret lost, he was contractually obligated to never again wrestle in the United States. Making matters worse for Bret, Shawn Michaels was the special referee.

At the match, with 26 minutes gone, Bret used the ringpost to apply his sharpshooter on The Undertaker. As Michaels tried to break the hold, The Undertaker kicked Bret into Michaels, sending him to the arena floor. Minutes later, an enraged Michaels reentered the ring and swung a chair at Bret's head. Bret ducked and Michaels inadvertently hit The Undertaker. Bret went for the cover, and Michaels realized he had no choice but to make the three-count.

And that's how Bret won his fifth and final WWF World title.

A year earlier, Bret had been offered a reported $9 million over three years to leave the WWF and join World Championship Wrestling (WCW), the WWF's staunchest rival. The WWF didn't want to lose Bret and it offered him a 20-year contract to stay. Bret opted for loyalty and stayed with the WWF, saying he'd be in the WWF forever.

Forever didn't last very long.

According to Bret's version of the story, in the fall of 1997, he received a call from McMahon, who said he wanted to break the contract. The WWF, McMahon said, couldn't afford him anymore. Stunned and disturbed, Bret talked things over with his wife, then called WCW to see if the old offer was still good. It was. Bret gave his notice to the WWF. He was leaving.

But there was one order of unfinished business. Bret was scheduled to defend the World title against Michaels at the 1997 Survivor Series.

This was a difficult situation for both sides. On the one hand, McMahon didn't want Hart to leave the federation with the belt. On the other hand, Bret wanted to protect his reputation. He wasn't simply going to lay down and lose to Michaels.

But that's exactly what McMahon wanted Bret to do. Even worse, he wanted Bret to do it at the Survivor Series, in Montreal, in front of Bret's adoring Canadian fans.

Bret refused to lose on purpose; McMahon apparently gave Bret his word that there would be no chicanery in the match.

Nobody knows exactly how things transpired at the Survivor Series, but this much is certain: only three seconds after Michaels locked Bret in a sharpshooter, referee Earl Hebner called for the bell and declared that Hart had submitted. Bret was furious. He stormed back to the dressing room and, according to witnesses, punched McMahon several times.

Sting puts NWO member Bret Hart in a chokehold. Since joining the NWO, Hart has feuded with Sting, "Diamond" Dallas Page, and "Rowdy" Roddy Piper.

"What he did with me in the Survivor Series was a total lack of respect for my fans, my fellow wrestlers, and me," Bret said. "I worked 14 years and gave this man the greatest performance in the history of the game, having missed only two shows in 14 years"

Bret had no choice but to move on to a new federation and a new life. When he arrived in WCW, it appeared as if Bret had again changed his ways and gone back to being a fan favorite. But he eventually sided with the New World Order (NWO), the most nefarious rulebreaking organization in the federation. As had happened before, Bret was angry with the fans for siding with wrestlers he viewed as bad role models. He did something once seemingly unthinkable: he sided with Hulk Hogan, a man he had detested in the WWF.

Bret has had his ups and downs in WCW. He has won three U.S. titles. He has feuded with such fan favorites as Sting, "Diamond" Dallas Page, and Roddy Piper, who beat him for the U.S. belt on February 8, 1999. He never officially joined the NWO, and when the group streamlined itself at Starrcade '98, Bret was left behind.

In May of 1999, Bret and the entire Hart family suffered a terrible loss. Bret's brother Owen was killed during a stunt at a WWF event when the high-wire harness he was wearing broke open, causing him to fall from the rafters of a wrestling arena. In a moving tribute to his younger brother that was published in the *Calgary Sun*, Bret wrote that the Hart family has always been admired for its strength, and that they must find the strength to go on without Owen. After 23 years of wrestling, Bret Hart has experienced more than one lifetime's share of successes, joys, and pains. His family is legendary, and Bret Hart is a legend too.

Chronology

1957 Born in Calgary, Alberta, on July 2.

1976 Makes his pro wrestling debut in Calgary with Stampede Wrestling.

1984 Joins the WWF after his father, Stu Hart, sells his Calgary wrestling territory to Vince McMahon Jr.

1987 With Jim Neidhart as his partner in the Hart Foundation, wins the WWF World tag team title.

1990 Wins second WWF World tag team title with Jim Neidhart.

1991 Beats Curt Hennig for the WWF Intercontinental title.

1992 Loses the WWF Intercontinental title to the Mountie at Royal Rumble.
Beats Roddy Piper at WrestleMania VII for a second Intercontinental title.
Loses the Intercontinental title at SummerSlam to Davey Boy Smith.
Beats Ric Flair for his first WWF World title in Saskatoon, Saskatchewan.

1993 Loses the WWF World title at WrestleMania IX to Yokozuna.

1994 Wins his second WWF World title at WrestleMania X from Yokozuna.
Loses the WWF World title at Survivor Series to Bob Backlund.

1995 Wins his third WWF World title at Survivor Series from Diesel.

1996 Loses the WWF World title at WrestleMania XIII to Shawn Michaels.

1997 Wins his fourth WWF World title in a four-way match for the vacant belt.
Loses the WWF World title one day later to Sid Vicious.
Wins his fifth WWF World title at SummerSlam from The Undertaker.
Loses the WWF World title to Shawn Michaels and leaves the federation.

1998 Wins his first, second, and third WCW U.S. titles.

1999 Loses his brother, Owen, in a tragic wrestling accident.

Further Reading

Burkett, Harry. "Bret Hart Gets a Title Gift from Shawn Michaels."
The Wrestler Digest (Spring 1998): 42–47.

Ricciuti, Edward R. *Face to Face with Bret "Hitman" Hart.* Woodbridge, CT:
Blackbirch Press, 1994.

Rodriguez, Andy. "Bret Hart: Cheating Himself out of Respect."
The Wrestler (January 1999): 38–41.

Rosenbaum, Dave. "Bret Screws Bret, Part II." *Pro Wrestling Illustrated*
(October 1998): 26–29.

"Press Conference: Bret Hart." *Pro Wrestling Illustrated* (November 1998):
22–23.

An interesting Bret Hart web site packed with articles can be found at:
http://www.canoe.ca/SlamWrestlingBretHart/home.html

Bret Hart also writes a regular column for the *Calgary Sun* newspaper.

Index

Abdullah the Butcher, 17
Andre the Giant, 23
Archie the Stomper, 17
Austin, Steve, 53–56
Backlund, Bob, 48
Bad News Brown, 28
Barbarian, the, 8
Bigelow, Bam Bam, 37, 40
Big Van Vader, 54
British Bulldogs, 25, 34
Calgary Hitmen, 51
Davis, Danny, 25
Demolition, 28
DiBiase, Ted, 29, 37
Diesel, 46, 49, 50
Dino Bravo, 8, 28
Dynamite Kid, 25
Elizabeth, 10
Ernest Manning High
  School, Calgary, 18
Flair, Ric, 35, 36
Gorilla Monsoon, 54
Hacksaw Duggan, 28
Hart, Alexandra, 51
Hart, Black, 51
Hart, Bret,
  birth, 16
  British Commonwealth
    mid-heavyweight title,
    21
  childhood, 15–19
  nicknamed "The
    Hitman," 22
  Stampede International
    tag team title, 21
  Stampede North
    American heavyweight
    titles, 22
  in WCW, 57–59
  WWC Caribbean tag
    team title, 21
  in WWF, 7–13, 23–57
  WWF Intercontinental
    title, 12, 13, 31, 33

WWF World heavyweight
  titles, 36, 46, 49, 56
WWF World tag team
  titles, 7, 25
Hart, Bruce, 10–13, 16, 43,
  44, 48
Hart, Dallas, 51
Hart, Dean, 16, 29
Hart, Diana, 21, 34, 35
Hart, Georgia, 18
Hart, Helen, 10, 12, 15–17, 48
Hart, Jade, 51
Hart, Jimmy, 23–26, 28,
  29, 32
Hart, Julie, 51
Hart, Keith, 16, 21, 43, 44
Hart, Owen, 16, 40, 43–48,
  55, 59
Hart, Ross, 16
Hart, Smith, 16, 21
Hart, Stu, 10, 12, 15–18,
  22, 23, 37, 44, 48
Hart, Wayne, 16
Hart Foundation, the, 7, 8,
  24–26, 28, 29, 31, 34, 55
Hearns, Tommy, 22
Hebner, Dave, 11, 38
Hebner, Earl, 57
Hennig, Curt, 9–13, 31, 40
Hennig, Larry, 9
Hogan, Hulk, 21, 23, 36,
  38–40, 59
Iron Sheik, the, 23
Jannetty, Marty, 28, 29
Kamala, 37
Lauper, Cyndi, 23
Lawler, Jerry, 40, 41, 43, 49
Luger, Lex, 45, 46
Martel, Rick, 26
Michaels, Shawn, 28, 29,
  33, 34, 37, 43, 46, 50, 51,
  53, 55–57
McMahon, Vince, Jr., 54, 57
McMahon, Vince, Sr., 22, 23

Mr. Fuji, 37, 38, 40
Mr. T, 23
Mountie, the, 32
Nash, Kevin, 21
Nasty Boys, the, 8, 29
National Wrestling Alliance
  (NWA), 35
Neidhart, Jim, 7, 8, 24–26,
  28, 29, 31, 46–48, 56
New World Order (NWO),
  58, 59
Pillman, Brian, 56
Piper, Roddy, 32, 33, 59
Quebecers, the, 44
Razor Ramon, 37, 40, 46, 47
Rougeua, Jacques, 25, 28
Rougeau, Raymond, 25,
  26, 28
Sammartino, Bruno, 23, 36
Santana, Tito, 25, 26
Savage, Randy, 10
Schyster, Irwin R., 8
Smith, Davey Boy, 21, 25,
  34, 35, 48, 49, 55
Stampede Wrestling, 10,
  21, 22
Tolos, John, 12
Tunney, Jack, 26, 29, 45, 50
Undertaker, The, 49, 50,
  54, 56
United States Wrestling
  Alliance (USWA), 41
Vicious, Sid, 54, 56
Warlord, the, 8
World Championship
  Wrestling (WCW), 56,
  58, 59
World Wrestling Council
  (WWC), 21
World Wrestling Federation
  (WWF), 7–9, 18, 23, 25, 26,
  28, 29, 31, 32, 34–36, 40,
  44–46, 48, 49, 53–57, 59
Yokozuna, 21, 37, 38, 40, 46

Photo Credits

All-Star Sports: p. 2; Jeff Eisenberg Sports Photography: pp. 6, 10, 14, 19, 20, 24, 27, 34, 39, 42, 44, 47, 48, 50, 55, 60; Sports Action: pp. 30, 58; WCW: p. 52.

JACQUELINE MUDGE is a frequent contributor to sports and entertainment magazines in the United States. Born in Idaho, she became a wrestling fan at age 11 when her father took her to matches. Although she has a degree in journalism, she left the writing arena for several years in the late-1980s to pursue a career in advertising sales. She returned to the profession—and the sport she loves—in 1995, and is now a correspondent for wrestling magazines around the world.